Come to Me!
The Story of Jesus and the Children

We are grateful to the following team of authors for their contributions to *God Loves Me*, a Bible story program for young children. This Bible story, one of a series of fifty-two, was written by Patricia L. Nederveld, managing editor for CRC Publications. Suggestions for using this book were developed by Sherry Ten Clay, training coordinator for CRC Publications and freelance author from Albuquerque, New Mexico. Yvonne Van Ee, an early childhood educator, served as project consultant and wrote *God Loves Me*, the program guide that accompanies this series of Bible storybooks.

Nederveld has served as a consultant to Title I early childhood programs in Colorado. She has extensive experience as a writer, teacher, and consultant for federally funded preschool, kindergarten, and early childhood programs in Colorado, Texas, Michigan, Florida, Missouri, and Washington, using the *High/Scope* Education Research Foundation curriculum. In addition to writing the *Bible Footprints* church curriculum for four- and five-year-olds, Nederveld edited the revised *Threes* curriculum and the first edition of preschool through second grade materials for the *LiFE* curriculum, all published by CRC Publications.

Ten Clay taught preschool for ten years in public schools in California, Missouri, and North Carolina and served as a Title IV preschool teacher consultant in Kansas City. For over twenty-five years she has served as a church preschool leader and also as a MOPS (Mothers of Preschoolers) volunteer. Ten Clay is coauthor of the preschool-kindergarten materials of the *LiFE* curriculum published by CRC Publications.

Van Ee is a professor and early childhood program advisor in the Education Department at Calvin College, Grand Rapids, Michigan. She has served as curriculum author and consultant for Christian Schools International and wrote the original *Story Hour* organization manual and curriculum materials for fours and fives.

Photos on page 5 and 20: Digital Stock Images.

© 1998 by CRC Publications, 2850 Kalamazoo Ave. SE, Grand Rapids, MI 49560. All rights reserved. With the exception of brief excerpts for review purposes, no part of this book may be reproduced in any manner whatsoever without written permission from the publisher. Printed in the United States of America on recycled paper. ✸ 1-800-333-8300

"God Loves Me" is a registered trademark of CRC Publications.

Library of Congress Cataloging-in-Publication Data

Nederveld, Patricia L., 1944-
    Come to me!: the story of Jesus and the children/Patricia L. Nederveld.
       p. cm. — (God loves me; bk. 40)
    Summary: Jesus blesses the children in this simple retelling of the Bible story. Includes follow-up activities.
    ISBN 1-56212-309-2
    1. Jesus Christ—Blessing of children—Juvenile literature.
[1. Jesus Christ—Blessing of children   2. Bible stories—N.T.]
I. Title.   II. Series: Nederveld, Patricia L., 1944-   God loves me bk. 40.
BT590.C48N43   1998
232.9'5—dc21
                                                                       98-15643
                                                                        CIP
                                                                         AC

10 9 8 7 6 5 4 3 2 1

Come to Me!
The Story of Jesus and the Children

PATRICIA L. NEDERVELD

ILLUSTRATIONS BY PATRICK KELLEY

CRC Publications
Grand Rapids, Michigan

This is a story from God's book, the Bible.

It's for _{say name(s) of your child(ren).} It's for me too!

Mark 10:13-16

Moms who love Jesus want their children to love Jesus too. Dads who love Jesus know that Jesus loves boys and girls very much!

Long ago, when Jesus lived on earth, some moms and dads took their boys and girls to see him. "Maybe Jesus will hug our children and tell them stories. What a wonderful time that would be!" they thought.

They did find Jesus! But he was very busy teaching grown-ups. The moms and dads and boys and girls waited. Would Jesus be happy to see them? Would he have time to talk to children too?

Jesus' helpers thought Jesus was far too busy to play with children. "Go away! Don't bother Jesus today. He's busy!" they said.

But Jesus didn't feel too busy. "Don't tell the children to go away! I want them to come to me. Don't you know that boys and girls are an important part of God's family?" Then Jesus smiled at the children.

The boys and girls smiled back at Jesus. They climbed onto his lap. They listened to his stories. They could tell that Jesus loved them. Everyone had a wonderful time—especially Jesus!

That day everyone knew that Jesus loves children. Jesus' helpers knew. The moms knew. The dads knew too. And best of all, each little girl and each little boy knew that Jesus loves children very much!

I wonder if you know that Jesus loves you very much . . .

Dear Jesus, thank you for loving moms and dads, boys and girls, and babies too. We love you, Jesus. Amen.

Suggestions for Follow-up

Opening

From the time your little ones arrive until they leave, look for chances to speak with each child. Greet them with a hug or a soft touch, and tell them how much Jesus loves them.

As you gather your group around you, take a moment to welcome each child by name. Tell the group that this is a child that Jesus loves! Or if your children can all speak fairly clearly, whisper "Jesus loves you!" around the circle, asking each child to pass it to the next.

Learning Through Play

Learning through play is the best way! The following activity suggestions are meant to help you provide props and experiences that will invite the children to play their way into the Scripture story and its simple truth. Try to provide plenty of time for the children to choose their own activities and to play individually. Use group activities sparingly—little ones learn most comfortably with a minimum of structure.

1. Encourage lots of pretending today. Make sure to bring dolls and other props to help children take the roles of mommies and daddies. Talk about how much Jesus loves grown-ups and children.

2. In your art area, provide glue sticks and pictures of children cut from magazines or catalogs. At the top of a large sheet of posterboard, write: Jesus Loves Children. Invite your little ones to help you make a collage of pictures. Admire each child pictured, and affirm the uniqueness of each of your helpers. (If you prefer, provide sheets of construction paper for each child to make a collage to take home.)

3. Sing or say "There's No One Exactly Like Me" (Songs Section, *God Loves Me* program guide) as children mimic your actions:

   Some children are short, and some children are tall. (hold hand open; low, then high)
   God loves us all, God loves us all. (point up, then cross arms over heart)
   Some children are short, and some children are tall. (hold hand open; low, then high)
   But no one's exactly like me. (shake head no, point to self)

   Some faces are dark, and some faces are light. (gently touch both cheeks)
   Each one is special (pat self on chest with open palm)
   in God's loving sight. (point up)
   Some faces are dark, and some faces are light. (gently touch both cheeks)
   But no one's exactly like me. (shake head no, point to self)

   —Words: adapted from lyrics by Trilby Jordan, © 1975, Broadman Press. All rights reserved. International copyright secured. Used by permission.

4. If your little ones enjoy games, here's one you might try together. Gather the children around you and tell them you are thinking about someone—someone Jesus loves very much. Tell them you will help them guess who that

someone is. Then describe one of the children in your group. Ask the children to look all around and find the person you're thinking of. When they guess correctly, invite the group to say, "Jesus loves you." Continue in this way until each of the children have been described, identified by the group, and assured of Jesus' love. (If you have helpers, include them in your game to help your little ones learn that Jesus loves grown-ups too!)

Closing

Take time to sing "Jesus Loves Me" (Songs Section, *God Loves Me* program guide) today. Close by praying for each child by name as you go around the circle and gently touch or hug each one.

At Home

Home is the first place where little ones begin to learn how important they are to Jesus—and to their family. Play this repetition game during your daily ride in the car or walk around the neighborhood or during bath time. Ask your little one, "Guess who loves you very much?" Then name a friend or family member. Repeat the question several times, each time adding a new name. Add Jesus' name to the list each time you play. After you've played the game a few times, your little one will remember the names too and may want to add new ones. Encourage your child to ask someone else in your family the "guess who" question.

Old Testament Stories

Blue and Green and Purple Too! *The Story of God's Colorful World*
It's a Noisy Place! *The Story of the First Creatures*
Adam and Eve *The Story of the First Man and Woman*
Take Good Care of My World! *The Story of Adam and Eve in the Garden*
A Very Sad Day *The Story of Adam and Eve's Disobedience*
A Rainy, Rainy Day *The Story of Noah*
Count the Stars! *The Story of God's Promise to Abraham and Sarah*
A Girl Named Rebekah *The Story of God's Answer to Abraham*
Two Coats for Joseph *The Story of Young Joseph*
Plenty to Eat *The Story of Joseph and His Brothers*
Safe in a Basket *The Story of Baby Moses*
I'll Do It! *The Story of Moses and the Burning Bush*
Safe at Last! *The Story of Moses and the Red Sea*
What Is It? *The Story of Manna in the Desert*
A Tall Wall *The Story of Jericho*
A Baby for Hannah *The Story of an Answered Prayer*
Samuel! Samuel! *The Story of God's Call to Samuel*
Lions and Bears! *The Story of David the Shepherd Boy*
David and the Giant *The Story of David and Goliath*
A Little Jar of Oil *The Story of Elisha and the Widow*
One, Two, Three, Four, Five, Six, Seven! *The Story of Elisha and Naaman*
A Big Fish Story *The Story of Jonah*
Lions, Lions! *The Story of Daniel*

New Testament Stories

Jesus Is Born! *The Story of Christmas*
Good News! *The Story of the Shepherds*
An Amazing Star! *The Story of the Wise Men*
Waiting, Waiting, Waiting! *The Story of Simeon and Anna*
Who Is This Child? *The Story of Jesus in the Temple*
Follow Me! *The Story of Jesus and His Twelve Helpers*
The Greatest Gift *The Story of Jesus and the Woman at the Well*
A Father's Wish *The Story of Jesus and a Little Boy*
Just Believe! *The Story of Jesus and a Little Girl*
Get Up and Walk! *The Story of Jesus and a Man Who Couldn't Walk*
A Little Lunch *The Story of Jesus and a Hungry Crowd*
A Scary Storm *The Story of Jesus and a Stormy Sea*
Thank You, Jesus! *The Story of Jesus and One Thankful Man*
A Wonderful Sight! *The Story of Jesus and a Man Who Couldn't See*
A Better Thing to Do *The Story of Jesus and Mary and Martha*
A Lost Lamb *The Story of the Good Shepherd*
Come to Me! *The Story of Jesus and the Children*
Have a Great Day! *The Story of Jesus and Zacchaeus*
I Love You, Jesus! *The Story of Mary's Gift to Jesus*
Hosanna! *The Story of Palm Sunday*
The Best Day Ever! *The Story of Easter*
Goodbye—for Now *The Story of Jesus' Return to Heaven*
A Prayer for Peter *The Story of Peter in Prison*
Sad Day, Happy Day! *The Story of Peter and Dorcas*
A New Friend *The Story of Paul's Conversion*
Over the Wall *The Story of Paul's Escape in a Basket*
A Song in the Night *The Story of Paul and Silas in Prison*
A Ride in the Night *The Story of Paul's Escape on Horseback*
The Shipwreck *The Story of Paul's Rescue at Sea*

Holiday Stories

Selected stories from the New Testament to help you celebrate the Christian year

Jesus Is Born! *The Story of Christmas*
Good News! *The Story of the Shepherds*
An Amazing Star! *The Story of the Wise Men*
Hosanna! *The Story of Palm Sunday*
The Best Day Ever! *The Story of Easter*
Goodbye—for Now *The Story of Jesus' Return to Heaven*

These fifty-two books are the heart of *God Loves Me*, a Bible story program designed for young children. Individual books (or the entire set) and the accompanying program guide *God Loves Me* are available from CRC Publications (1-800-333-8300).